DATE DUE

Getting To Know...

Nature's Children

WOODCHUCKS

Laima Dingwall

PUBLISHER	Joseph R. DeVarennes	
PUBLICATION DIRECTOR	Kenneth H. Pearson	
MANAGING EDITOR	Valerie Wyatt	
SERIES ADVISOR	Merebeth Switzer	
SERIES CONSULTANT	Michael Singleton	
CONSULTANTS	Ross James	
	Kay McKeever	
	Dr. Audrey N. Tomera	
ADVISORS	Roger Aubin	
	Robert Furlonger	
	Gaston Lavoie	
EDITORIAL SUPERVISOR	Jocelyn Smyth	
PRODUCTION MANAGER	Ernest Homewood	
PRODUCTION ASSISTANTS	Penelope Moir	
	Brock Piper	
EDITORS	Katherine Farris	Anne Minguet-Patocka
	Sandra Gulland	Sarah Reid
	Cristel Kleitsch	Cathy Ripley
	Elizabeth MacLeod	Eleanor Tourtel
	Pamela Martin	Karin Velcheff
PHOTO EDITORS	Bill Ivy	
	Don Markle	
DESIGN	Annette Tatchell	
CARTOGRAPHER	Jane Davie	
PUBLICATION ADMINISTRATION	Kathy Kishimoto	
	Monique Lemonnier	
ARTISTS	Marianne Collins	Greg Ruhl
	Pat Ivy	Mary Theberge

This series is approved and recommended by the Federation of Ontario Naturalists.

Canadian Cataloguing in Publication Data

Dingwall, Laima, 1953-
  Woodchucks

(Getting to know—nature's children)
Includes index.
ISBN 0-7172-1905-4

1. Marmots—Juvenile literature.
I. Title.   II. Series.

QL737.R68D56 1985   j599.32'32   C85-098745-8

Have you ever wondered . . .

How much wood
would a woodchuck chuck
if a woodchuck could chuck wood?
Almost everybody knows this famous tongue twister, even if they have trouble saying it. But the woodchuck has another claim to fame.

Woodchucks are also called groundhogs, and, in North America, they have their own special day: February 2. Each year on that day, so the legend goes, the groundhog comes out of the den where it has been sleeping away the winter. If it sees its shadow, it will be frightened and dive back into its den to sleep for another six weeks. That means there will be six more weeks of winter. If the groundhog does not see its shadow, spring should be on the way.

What is this star of rhymes and weather reports really like? It is a furry, fuzzy, roly-poly ground squirrel that loves to stuff itself with fresh greens and bask in the warm sun.

Opposite page:

Woodchucks are curious and will often sit at the entrance to their den and study their surroundings.

Family Fun

A baby woodchuck spends its days eating and playing with its brothers and sisters. They wrestle and roll onto their backs. They may even chase each other round and round in circles. Then they start all over again! When the little woodchucks finally tire themselves out, they stretch out and bask in the warm sun.

As the young woodchucks grow up they must learn how to dig dens, protect themselves from predators and much more.

The woodchuck often digs the entrance to its den at the base of a tree.

Woodchuck Relatives

No one is quite sure how the woodchuck got the name groundhog. Maybe it was because its squat, fat body reminded some people of a round, fur-covered pig. In fact, pioneers called it the whistle pig because it makes a loud whistling noise when frightened.

Actually the woodchuck is not a pig at all. It is a type of marmot, which is a ground-dwelling squirrel. It is related to other squirrels, chipmunks and Prairie Dogs.

However the woodchuck looks quite different from its relatives. For one thing, it is the biggest North American squirrel. A full-grown woodchuck may be as long as 60 centimetres (24 inches) from the tip of its nose to the end of its bushy tail. And it may weigh between two and five kilograms (5-11 pounds). That's about the same size as an average house cat. Female woodchucks are slightly smaller than males.

Opposite page:

Did you know the woodchuck is a rodent? Only two other North American rodents are bigger—the beaver and the porcupine.

9

Woodchuck Country

Opposite page:

Out on a limb.

Woodchucks are found over much of North America. They are most common in the east, from the southern United States to Hudson Bay, but they are also found right across the prairies to the west coast and as far north as the Yukon and central Alaska.

You will find some woodchucks living in open fields or clearings, but most live on the edge of forests. There they have places to hide from enemies and a wide variety of foods to eat.

Where woodchucks live.

10

Sizing Up the Territory

How many woodchucks live in the same clearing or forest edge? That depends on the amount of food in the area and the number of predators who also live there. If there is lots of food, then there may be as many as five woodchucks per half hectare (1 acre). But if the food supply is low, or there are many predators, only a few woodchucks will live in the same area. Usually a woodchuck has a territory of about two hectares (5 acres).

There is certainly enough tender grass here for these two woodchucks to share.

The Warm Woolly Woodchuck

The woodchuck looks its best in the late fall when its winter coat has grown in. This coat is made up of two layers. An inner layer of thick, woolly fur holds in the woodchuck's body heat, while the longer, stiff guard hairs keep out wind and wet. These guard hairs lie flat and smooth over the underfur so water runs right off.

Most woodchucks are medium brown in color. However some may be straw yellow, while others are dark reddish brown or any color in between. No matter what the body color, the woodchuck's feet and tail are almost always black or dark brown.

This woodchuck looks very handsome in its fine two-tone fall coat.

What a Salad Lover

Do you like salads? If so, you have something in common with the woodchuck. It loves fresh greens, but it will eat almost any plants it can find. Among its favorites are clover, alfalfa, buckwheat, buttercups and goldenrod. But it also feasts on farm crops such as corn, beets, celery, lettuce, cabbage and turnips. No wonder some farmers and gardeners think the woodchuck is a pest! When tender greens are scarce, the woodchuck will eat other plant material, even bark and twigs. It might also munch on insects or snails.

The woodchuck usually feeds during the daytime. In the early spring, it does most of its eating during the warmest part of the day, around noon. But in the summer when the sun is very hot, the woodchuck eats at the coolest times of the day, just after dawn and again just before dusk.

Woodchucks love dandelions—flower, leaves, stem and all.

On the Lookout

While the woodchuck is munching away on plants, it often pauses to sit up and look around. No, it is not taking a rest from eating. It is taking a quick but thorough look around to make sure there are no predators lurking nearby.

Sometimes, after a meal, the woodchuck will drape itself over a pile of smooth rocks or around a fence and soak up some sun. But even when it is sunbathing it is always listening and watching for any sign of trouble.

When out in the open, the woodchuck is always on the alert, and it will try to stay within dashing-distance of its hole.

Danger! Danger!

The Red Fox, coyote and the eagle are the woodchuck's main predators. Its best defences against them are its keen senses of sight and hearing. That is why a woodchuck in the open remains constantly alert. If it senses an enemy, it dashes for its burrow and dives in. But as it does so, it gives a shrill whistle. This whistle warns any nearby woodchucks: "Be careful! Danger may be close at hand."

Quite an Athlete

Do not be fooled by the woodchuck's short legs or by its unusual rather poky walk. It can speed along at up to 17 kilometres (10 miles) per hour if it is being chased. That is about as fast as you might race through a field.

The woodchuck is also a good swimmer and a good climber and often climbs trees and fenceposts to observe the countryside.

Sounding the alarm!

Stand and Fight

Foxes and coyotes are in for an unpleasant surprise if they manage to corner a woodchuck. Instead of a meek plump ball of fur, they find themselves face to face with a fierce fighter.

Before it fights, the woodchuck tries to scare off the enemy. It opens its mouth wide to show its sharp teeth. It may even grind them together to make a scraping sound. Many enemies would rather give up than fight such a ferocious looking opponent.

If that does not work, the woodchuck will fight the enemy, even one that is many times bigger than it is. Then—watch out! The woodchuck's bite can be painful; its teeth are almost as big and strong as a beaver's.

A woodchuck will usually dive into its hole to escape an enemy. Once safely inside it may peek out and show off its teeth as a threat.

A Smart Builder

Like their cousins the Prairie Dogs, woodchucks live in underground dens, or burrows. Sometimes they even have two dens—one for summer and the other for their winter hibernation. Often the summer den is out in a field or clearing, while the hibernating den is hidden in the woods.

The den is dug in well-drained soil so that it will stay dry. The woodchuck starts by digging a tunnel. Then it hollows out a sleeping room and often a separate toilet room too. The older the woodchuck the more elaborate this den will be. Some dens have several entrances and chambers and wide tunnels.

Most dens also have a secret tunnel called a ''plunge hole.'' This is a tunnel that leads straight down instead of sloping gently into the den as most of the tunnels do. If the woodchuck is being chased by a hungry predator it simply plunges into this hole and seems to disappear. The pursuer is left wondering where its dinner went.

Opposite page:

A young woodchuck is not afraid of hard work. On a single day it can dig a burrow a metre and a half (5 feet) long and 10 centimetres (4 inches) wide.

25

Digging Machine

Tunneling into the ground is easy for a woodchuck. It has powerful legs and long, curved claws that are perfect for digging. Each front paw has four claws and each back foot has five claws.

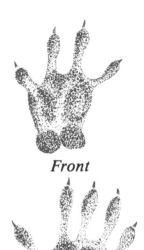

Front

Hind

Woodchuck paw prints.

When it is working on its den, the woodchuck digs with its front paws and kicks the loose dirt backwards with its back paws. This hard worker does not even slow down if it comes face to face with a big rock. It simply pushes the rock out using its flat, wide head almost like a bulldozer. And if the woodchuck meets a fat tree root in its digging, it clips the root in half using its sharp front teeth.

The woodchuck is such a super digger that in its lifetime it can move enough soil and rocks to fill an entire railway freight car. Now that's a lot of digging!

A Good Housekeeper

The woodchuck cleans out its den regularly and keeps the den's tunnels clear of dirt. In fact, you can often spot the entrance to a woodchuck's tunnel by the mound of soil around it.

Some woodchucks line the floor of their sleeping rooms with leaves and grass to make themselves a comfortable bed. In the summer this "bedding" is changed from time to time, just as you change the sheets on your bed. But in winter woodchucks cannot change the grass and leaves. Why not? They are too busy sleeping.

Wintertime Woodchuck

The woodchuck gets ready for winter by stuffing itself with food. By late fall it has gained so much weight that it lumbers along as it runs. When food begins to become scarce, the now roly-poly woodchuck waddles down into the sleeping room of its den. It plugs up all the entrances with earth and straw and does not show itself again until the early spring.

Inside its cozy grass-lined sleeping room, the woodchuck rolls itself into a tight little ball with its head tucked between its back legs. Gradually its heart rate slows down from the normal 80 beats per minute to just 4 or 5 beats per minute. Its breathing slows down too. The woodchuck now takes only one breath every 6 minutes. Its body temperature also drops to just a few degrees above freezing.

In this very deep hibernation sleep, the woodchuck lives through the coldest months of the year. It does not even have to wake up to eat. By slowing down its breathing and heart rate it uses less energy and can live off its own fat.

Opposite page:

By late fall woodchucks are quite chubby. The extra fat they have put on will see them through their winter sleep.

Groundhog Day

People once thought that all woodchucks woke up on February 2, Groundhog Day. No one is sure how the woodchuck got mixed up with this superstition, but today we know that most woodchucks sleep right through their special day. Most do not wake up from their winter hibernation until March. Full-grown male woodchucks are usually the first ones up and around, followed, a few weeks later, by the full-grown females and the young woodchucks.

Opposite page:

After five or six months underground, it's good to see daylight again!

The woodchuck rolls up into a tight ball to sleep away the winter.

Waking Up

It takes a woodchuck several hours to wake up—and no wonder! After all, it has been sleeping soundly for up to six months!

Before the woodchuck leaves its den in the spring, several things happen. First its heart rate gradually speeds up until it is back to its usual 80 beats per minute. Then the woodchuck starts to breathe at a normal rate. Finally it uncurls its body and begins to shiver. The rapid shaking movements help warm it up, and at last the woodchuck is ready to leave its den. It digs out the straw and dirt plugging the exit from its sleeping room and wanders up the tunnel to the outdoors.

As you might imagine, the woodchuck is by now very hungry. It has used up its supply of stored fat during hibernation and now it must eat. But sometimes there is still snow covering the ground and the hungry woodchuck is forced to munch on the bark and twigs of trees, such as cherry, sumac and dogwood.

Pretty poor pickings!

Mating Time

Woodchucks mate soon after they come out of their den in the early spring. At mating time, the male woodchuck wanders great distances and may mate with several females. Two males may even fight quite fierce battles over a mate. These battles usually end before any serious damage is done, but many older males end up with quite a collection of scars.

Meet the Newborn Woodchuck

About a month after mating, the female woodchuck gives birth to a litter of four to six babies. They are born in a grass-lined sleeping room that serves as a nursery.

A newborn woodchuck is very tiny. It measures just 10 centimetres (4 inches) from the tip of its nose to the end of its tail. It weighs barely 26 grams (1 ounce). The babies are so small that you could probably hold the entire litter in your two cupped hands.

Baby woodchucks are born without any fur. They are pink and very wrinkly. Their eyes are not yet open and they cannot hear very well either.

This baby woodchuck is two or three weeks old. Its fur has grown in, but its eyes are not yet open.

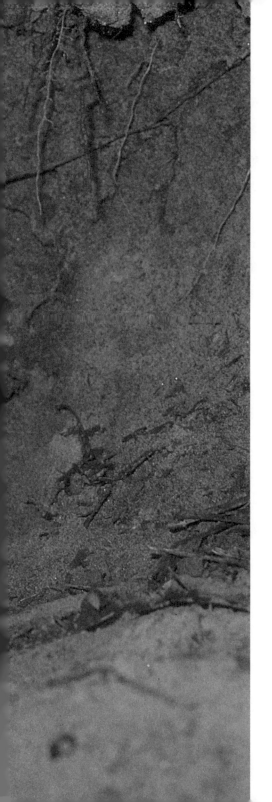

Mother Love

The female woodchuck must raise and feed her family alone. She looks after them very well, licking and cleaning them carefully and feeding them with her milk.

The mother stays very close to her babies during the night. But at daybreak, she leaves the burrow to find food for herself. Even then she always stays within hearing distance of her babies. That way she can return quickly if she senses danger.

Cheek to cheek.

Getting Stronger

By the time the baby woodchucks are two weeks old, they are covered with short, fuzzy fur. When they are about four weeks old, they open their eyes and start to crawl around the den. They might even try to follow their mother out of the den when she goes off to find food. But their baby legs are still weak, and they cannot yet manage the long walk up the tunnel to the outdoors. So, more often than not, the tiny woodchucks stagger back to the nursery and collapse in a tired heap.

But day by day the babies get stronger. When they are five or six weeks old they finally follow their mother out of the den. Imagine their surprise when they poke their little noses outside the den for the first time into the bright sunshine.

Stepping out.

Meeting the World Outside

Not long after the young woodchucks leave the
nursery for the first time they sample their
first solid food. They nibble on the plants and
other greenery around the entrance to the den
and gradually stop nursing on their mother's
milk. As they eat this new food the young
woodchucks grow very quickly. By the time
they are eight weeks old, they each weigh
about 1 kilogram (2 pounds).

Young woodchucks will reach their
full growth late in their second year.

On Their Own

By the time the young woodchucks get this big, life in the den is getting very crowded. It is time for them to leave home.

The young woodchuck's first task once it is on its own is to dig a den. Although this den is small and simple compared to its mother's den, it is still home. There the woodchuck will live until it is ready to have a family of its own. In the wild, woodchucks may live to be six years old and may have several families over the years.

And just in case you are still wondering how much wood a woodchuck *would* chuck:
It would chuck all the wood
that a woodchuck could
—if a woodchuck could chuck wood.

Special Words

Burrow   A hole dug in the ground by an animal for use as a home.

Den   Animal home.

Groundhog   Another name for the woodchuck.

Guard hairs   Long coarse hairs that make up the outer layer of the woodchuck's coat.

Hibernation   Deep sleep that some animals, including woodchucks, go into for the entire winter.

Litter   A family of young woodchucks.

Marmot   A burrowing rodent.

Nurse   To drink milk from a mother's body.

Plunge hole   A vertical den entrance that woodchucks run into to escape predators.

Predator   An animal that hunts others animals for food.

Rodent   An animal with teeth that are especially good for gnawing.

INDEX

Cover Photo: Brian Milne (Valan Photos)

Photo Credits: Bill Ivy, pages 4, 7, 8, 15, 16, 23, 24, 32, 35, 39, 40, 43, 44;
François Morneau (Valan Photos), page 11; M. J. Johnson (Valan Photos), page
12; Wayne Lankinen (Valan Photos), pages 19, 20; Albert Kuhnigk (Valan
Photos), page 27; Harold V. Green, page 31; Pat Ivy, page 36.

Getting To Know...

Nature's Children

ALLIGATORS

Melanie Zola
and
Katherine Grier

PUBLISHER	Joseph R. DeVarennes
PUBLICATION DIRECTOR	Kenneth H. Pearson
MANAGING EDITOR	Valerie Wyatt
SERIES ADVISOR	Merebeth Switzer
SERIES CONSULTANT	Michael Singleton
CONSULTANTS	Ross James
	Kay McKeever
	Dr. Audrey N. Tomera
ADVISORS	Roger Aubin
	Robert Furlonger
	Gaston Lavoie
EDITORIAL SUPERVISOR	Jocelyn Smyth
PRODUCTION MANAGER	Ernest Homewood
PRODUCTION ASSISTANTS	Penelope Moir
	Brock Piper

EDITORS

Katherine Farris	Anne Minguet-Patocka
Sandra Gulland	Sarah Reid
Cristel Kleitsch	Cathy Ripley
Elizabeth MacLeod	Eleanor Tourtel
Pamela Martin	Karin Velcheff

PHOTO EDITORS	Bill Ivy
	Don Markle
DESIGN	Annette Tatchell
CARTOGRAPHER	Jane Davie
PUBLICATION ADMINISTRATION	Kathy Kishimoto
	Monique Lemonnier

ARTISTS

Marianne Collins	Greg Ruhl
Pat Ivy	Mary Theberge

This series is approved and recommended by the Federation of Ontario Naturalists.

Canadian Cataloguing in Publication Data

Zola, Melanie, 1952-
  Alligators

(Getting to know—nature's children)
Includes index.
ISBN 0-7172-1906-2

1. Alligators—Juvenile literature.
I. Title. II. Series.

QL666.C925Z64 1985   j597.98   C85-098700-8

Have you ever wondered . . .

Have you ever seen an alligator swimming? If you have, you might have thought that its long, tapered body and rough bark-like skin looked a lot like a floating log. Or maybe its toothy jaws and armored scales reminded you of the dinosaurs that disappeared from the earth long ago.

For many years most people judged alligators by how they looked or by frightening stories other people told. Alligators seemed like monsters from the swamps. In some stories, they even breathed fire and smoke.

It is not easy to watch alligators in the wild: they are shy and good at hiding. But gradually naturalists have begun to sort the facts from the stories. They have found that alligators are not so different from other animals as they might seem. And like all living creatures, alligators are beautifully suited to play their own important part in the natural world.

The American Alligator is the largest reptile in North America.

Just What Are Alligators?

The Spanish were the first Europeans to explore the American south, where the American Alligator lives. They called the alligator "el lagarto," which means "giant lizard." (Run the Spanish words together and you will see where the name "alligator" comes from.)

But alligators are not really lizards at all. They are crocodilians. Their only close relatives are the crocodiles, the caimans of South and Central America and the gavial, which lives in India.

The Spanish had the right idea, however, because both crocodilians and lizards are reptiles.

Like other reptiles, alligators have tough, scaly skin, breathe air into their lungs and are cold-blooded. "Cold-blooded" does not mean that their blood is cold. It just means that the temperature around them affects their body temperature. They become warmer as the temperature outside rises and cooler as it falls.

Caimans are more closely related to alligators than crocodiles are. They are not native to North America, but, the Spectacled Caiman, seen here, has been introduced and seems to be establishing itself in southern Florida.

Crocodilian Who's Who

People often get the alligator and the crocodile mixed up. And, in fact, it can be difficult to look at one and be sure which it is. If you saw both together, however, it would be easier.

Alligator

The alligator has a broad, blunt snout. The crocodile, on the other hand, has a rather narrow snout that comes to more of a point at the tip. Also, in crocodiles the upper and lower teeth are more or less in line, and the large fourth lower tooth fits into a notch in the upper jaw. As a result this tooth remains visible even when the animal's mouth is closed. The alligator's lower teeth close inside the upper ones, and the large fourth lower tooth fits into a pit in the upper jaw. It cannot be seen when the alligator's mouth is closed.

Crocodile

Apart from these visible differences, there are differences of location and behavior. Crocodiles live only in the tropics. The only place they and alligators are found together is in the southernmost part of Florida. Finally alligators are less aggressive and they move more slowly than their crocodile relatives.

9

Alligator Country

Because alligators are cold-blooded, they cannot survive where the winters are very cold. In spite of this, they live much farther north than most of their crocodilian relatives.

The Chinese Alligator lives in the Yangtze River Valley in China, and the American Alligator can be found almost halfway up the east coast of the United States.

Where alligators live in North America.

Wet Homes

Alligators usually live in fresh water, but sometimes they are seen where fresh and salt water mix, at places where inland rivers or marshes meet the ocean. They prefer slow water to fast-moving water. And they avoid muddy water because it is hard to see and catch prey in the dark murkiness.

Alligators find slow, fresh, clear water in many places—in swamps, marshes, streams, lagoons, even in places where many small ponds lie close together.

Wherever they live, alligators are creatures of the shallows and shores. There they find their food. And there they find the conditions that help their bodies stay at a comfortable temperature.

A Thick Skin

The alligator's tough, blackish skin protects it from the roughness of the ground. Long ago, in the age of the dinosaurs, it probably also protected the alligator's ancestors from large enemies. Today those enemies no longer exist.

The alligator's skin is made up of rectangular scales. They run down its body in rows and are joined by narrow bands of heavy, wrinkled skin. The large scales on the alligator's back and neck look like armor. They rise into ridges in the center and are strengthened inside with small plates of bone. The scales on the alligator's belly are also tough. But they are smooth and flat, and they do not have bony plates inside them.

A rest in the sun.

On the Move

Opposite page:

"Do I smell dinner?"

An alligator's legs are short and its body is long and heavy. It looks as if it should be clumsy and slow.

But in the water, the alligator is graceful and fast. The alligator uses its short legs and webbed feet to steady itself in the water—just as you use your hands and arms to steady yourself when you float. To swim, it tucks its feet close to its body and sweeps its flat, heavy tail from side to side. At top speed, an alligator can move through the water much faster than a person paddling a canoe.

On land, the alligator is not quite as graceful. It can run quickly for short distances, but it tires quickly and must stop to rest. Even so, an alligator sometimes travels long distances overland to find a new home.

When an alligator walks, its short legs hold its body off the ground, but its tail drags along behind.

14

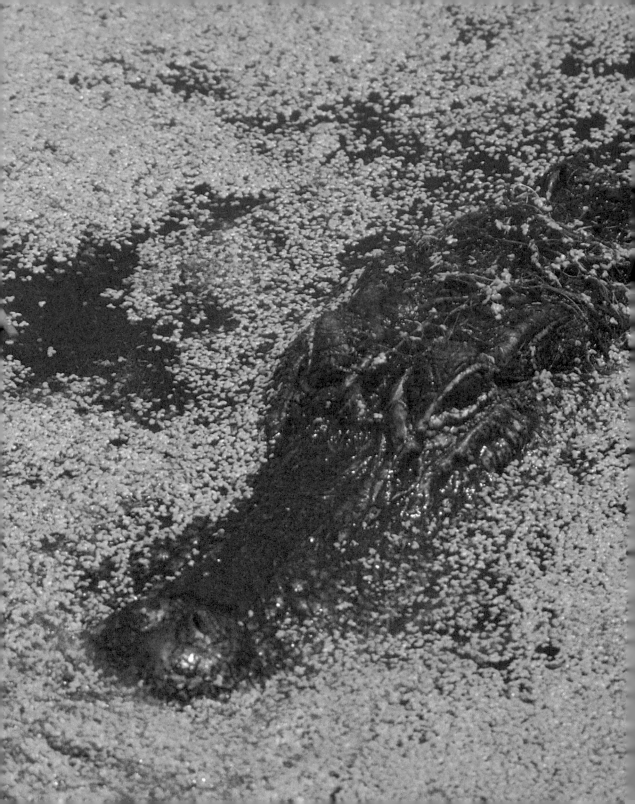

Under Water

When you swim underwater do you use a mask and snorkel? An alligator does not need to wear any special equipment. Its underwater equipment is built in!

To keep the water out of its eyes, the alligator has an extra eyelid which slides sideways over its eyes. The eyelid is clear so the alligator can see through it. Flaps of skin automatically close over the alligator's slit-like ears when it dives. And a system of muscles and fleshy flaps around the nostrils controls the intake of air and water so that it never accidentally gets a noseful or lungful.

Because alligators need to breathe in air through their noses, they have come up with a way of keeping their nose out of the water even when the rest of them is almost totally submerged. They have their nostrils high on the tip of their snouts. Sometimes all you can see when an alligator is swimming is the tip of its nose and its eyes.

Opposite page:

Danger lurks in the swamp for any unwary animal.

17

A Meaty Diet

Alligators are meat eaters. The kind of meat alligators eat depends on where they live. An alligator that lives on a riverbank will not find the same prey as one in a swamp or marsh.

Some of the alligator's prey live in the water—slow-moving fish, turtles and frogs. Some, such as water birds and snakes, swim or dive into the water to look for food. And others, such as muskrats, rabbits, young deer and raccoons, share the banks or shore with the alligator or come to the water's edge to drink. Very large alligators will even attack cows.

Alligators also swallow hard objects. No one is quite sure why, but some naturalists think that swallowed rocks or bones or chunks of wood help grind up the alligator's food. Others think that their weight helps the alligator keep its balance in the water.

Hunting by Surprise

Most of the time, an alligator does not travel very far to hunt. Instead it lies in one place, still and hidden, waiting to catch its prey by surprise. And it can hide very well. Its dark, rough body looks like a log. And as we have discovered, its nostrils and eyes are often the only things that show above the water.

No one is quite sure how an alligator first senses its prey—by smelling it, seeing it or feeling the vibrations its movements make. If its prey is not close enough to catch, the alligator stalks stealthily closer and closer. When its prey is within reach, it lunges forward and seizes it with a sideways snap of its jaws. If the prey puts up a fight, the alligator may pull it underwater and hold it there until it drowns.

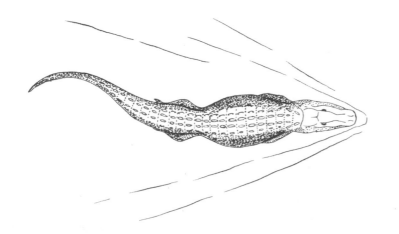

An alligator swims by sweeping its tail from side to side.

What a Mouthful

The alligator's jaws are ideal for grabbing and holding. They are lined with large, cone-shaped teeth. And powerful muscles snap them shut. But the alligator's pointed teeth are not well suited for chewing. Most of the time the alligator swallows its prey whole. If a catch is too big, it tears it into pieces that are small enough to swallow.

Alligators do not use up the energy in food as quickly as many other animals. This means they do not need to eat as much as you might expect. Sometimes an alligator will make a catch just because it is easy. Then it might hold the meal in its mouth for hours before feeling hungry enough to swallow.

Jaws!

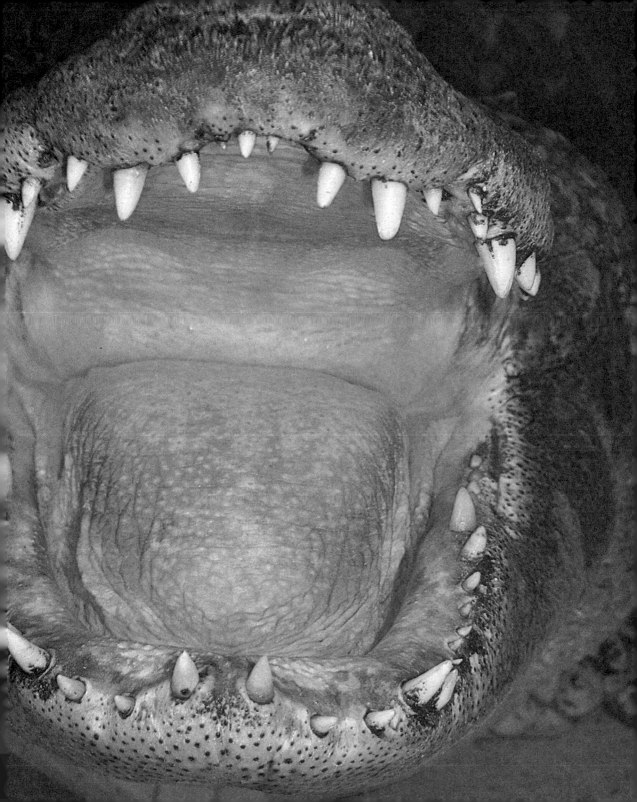

Trespassers Beware!

Each alligator has its own territory—a piece of land and water that it and no other adult alligator will consider its own. A younger alligator may have to seek a new and bigger territory several times as it grows larger and stronger. A full-grown one may use the same territory year after year.

Alligators rarely fight over territory. Instead they have safer ways of avoiding or settling arguments. By closing their mouth and forcing air out their nostrils, they make a deep roaring sound. When an alligator bellows over and over again from the same place, it is saying: "This place is already taken."

If an alligator enters an occupied territory, the owner lunges toward the intruder, hissing loudly and open-mouthed. Although the owner is putting on a show and not a real attack, the intruder usually leaves.

Staying Warm and Keeping Cool

An alligator spends much of its time keeping warm, but not too warm. It often spends the night in the water since the water has been warmed by the heat of the sun. By dawn, the night air will have cooled the water off. Then the alligator climbs out and warms itself in the sun on the shore.

When it gets too hot, an alligator cannot cool itself by sweating as you can. Instead it opens its jaws to let heat escape through the moist lining of its mouth. Or it finds a shady resting place in the water.

Alligators and puppy dogs may not seem to have much in common, but both pant to cool themselves off.

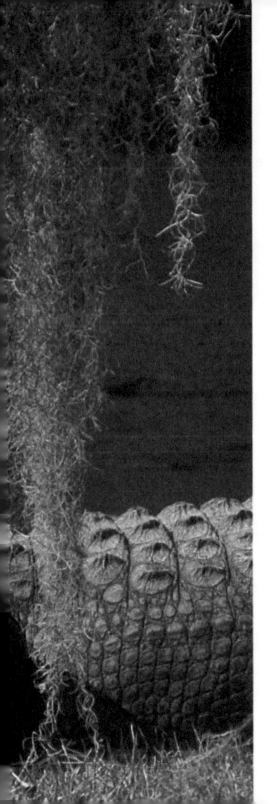

Coping with Winter

Alligators cannot survive cold northern winters, but some do live where the winters get very chilly. How do they manage?

In the early autumn, they dig shelters. Some clear a shelter among the roots at the edge of a river bank; others dig long, narrow tunnels into soft wet banks.

There the alligator spends the coldest months of the year. Its heart beats slowly, and its body uses up its food so slowly that it eats very little or nothing. Often it does not stir until warm weather returns.

On a warm winter day an alligator may venture out of its den to bask in the sun.

27

Staying Wet in the Dry Season

Alligators who live farther south do not have to worry about cold. Instead they must guard against the dry weather that winter sometimes brings. Dry weather may make the water level in their home pond or river drop. When this happens, the alligators may not be able to find enough food. How do alligators survive a dry spell?

While the water is still high from summer rains, they use their tails and bodies to wallow out and deepen part of their pond or marsh. They sweep the dark muck up from the bottom to make a round rim just below the water's surface. When the shallower water dries up, water is still left in the deeper "gator-hole." During the dry season, gator-holes become the center of life not only for the alligator. Many other creatures find them handy places to live and find food and drink.

Because water is slower to chill than air, the gator-hole also gives the alligator some protection against an unexpected cold spell.

Two lovestruck alligators.

Spring Mating

Spring is mating time for alligators. Naturalists are not sure how male and female alligators find one another. Some think they leave trails of scent on the ground which other alligators can follow. Both males and females seem to search for a mate, and if several males find one female, the female seems to do the choosing.

Once the female has chosen, the male follows her about, strokes her back and sometimes blows bubbles past her snout. After 3 to 17 days, the female is ready to mate. She lets the male fertilize the eggs she is carrying inside her. Now the eggs can develop into baby alligators. After the adults mate, they have nothing more to do with one another.

Building a Nest

In early June, about two months after mating, the female gets ready to build a nest.

She usually chooses a partly shady spot close to the water. The nest must be cool enough so that the eggs will not overheat and high enough that flood waters cannot reach them.

Using her body and tail, she makes a mound of earth, leaves and grasses. She works mostly at night, resting now and then. After several nights, she has built a mound about one metre (3 feet) wide and about as high as your thigh. She packs the mound down by crawling all over it. Finally she uses her hind feet to dig a hole in the top.

When the nest is ready, she lays her eggs in the hole at the top. Fully grown females may lay as many as 52 eggs, but most lay about 30. The eggs are bright white, the same shape at both ends and almost twice the size of a chicken egg.

When all the eggs are laid, the female carefully covers over the hole to keep the eggs safe and warm.

Opposite page:

There's plenty of nesting material here.

A Nest to Guard

Once the eggs are laid, it takes two or three months before the baby alligators are ready to hatch.

The female guards her nest, often resting her throat against it. If she senses a threat, she tries to scare the intruder away without really fighting. She lunges and hisses the same way alligators defend their territory.

Some naturalists think that the female stays by her nest and does not even leave to eat until the young have hatched. Others think that she watches carefully at first but eventually leaves to find food.

The female alligator stays close to her nest to discourage visitors.

Happy Hatchday

Having a tough protective shell is handy for the baby alligators. It keeps them safe as they grow inside it. But getting out of that tough shell at hatchtime can be a problem. The hatchlings cut their way out of their shells using a special "egg-tooth." This is not really a tooth. It is a hard tip on the end of their snouts that falls off soon after they hatch.

How do alligators get out of their mound nest? No one seems to know for sure. Some people think that their mother hears her young grunting inside their eggs before they hatch and uncovers the nest to help them out. Others say the grunts are so faint that she cannot hear them. They think baby alligators, like newly hatched turtles, climb out of the nest on their own.

A mother alligator may use her sharp claws and teeth to pull the nest mound apart so the hatchlings can get out.

Alligator Hatchlings

If you ever saw a baby alligator you might wonder how all that alligator fit into such a small shell. A baby alligator is about 22 centimetres (9 inches) long. That is longer than a new pencil.

It is shaped exactly like its parents, except that its belly sticks out with leftover egg yolk. It will feed on this yolk for its first few days. Its undersides are dull white, its back and sides blackish with wandering white lines. Within a week, the white turns to yellow and then gradually darkens until the young alligator has its blackish adult coloring.

The first thing a baby alligator does is make its way to the safety of the water. Some think the mother leads the way. Others think the babies hatch knowing which way to go.

On its own.

Early Life

Life is hard for a baby alligator. Great blue herons, hawks and other birds of prey, some snakes and the occasional fish or bullfrog find the hatchling an easy catch.

Adult alligators share the water and shore with the hatchlings, but the only time they pay attention to a young alligator is when it cries out shrilly over and over again. This is a distress call and the young alligator uses it only when it is seized by a predator. Any adult alligator who hears it rushes to the youngster's defense.

The rest of the time, the young alligator looks after itself. It finds its own shelter and catches its own food—water insects, spiders, tadpoles, crayfish or anything else that is smaller and slower than it is.

With all the dangers, it is not surprising that only one in ten baby alligators survives its first year.

Baby alligators are busy hunters. They eat minnows, tadpoles, crabs and aquatic insects.

Growing Up

A young alligator grows quickly. In its first year it may triple in length. After that it may grow as much as 30 centimetres (12 inches) a year. Exactly how fast an alligator grows seems to depend on how well it can feed and where it lives. Young alligators in a marsh full of waterlife grow faster than young alligators in swamps or rivers where the pickings are slimmer.

When an alligator is four years old, it is a little over one metre (3 feet) long. At this age it stops making the distress call and starts answering it instead. It is not yet fully grown, however. Instead it is like a teenager in the alligator world. About this time, adults start driving it off their territory, and it must set out to find a territory of its own. It begins to practice bellowing, sounding a little raspy at first.

Next season, when it is five, the young alligator will be ready to mate for the first time.

Long Lives

Although they are ready to mate when they are five, alligators continue to grow for several more years. They grow quickly until they are about eight years old. By then they are about two and three-quarters metres (9 feet) long. After that their growth slows down. Females grow only a little bit more. Some males stop growing at about four metres (13 feet) but get broader and heavier. Others stay slim but grow even longer—up to about five metres (16 feet).

As an alligator grows, its tough outer skin is shed in tiny flakes as new skin grows in underneath. The alligator's teeth, too, are constantly being replaced, and this will continue almost all through its life. Fortunately, the alligator does not lose its worn teeth all at once, so it is never completely toothless. The different ages of an alligator's teeth explain why some are big and some are small.

After an alligator reaches four or five, it has few enemies. It may live for many years—up to 50 for males and 30 for females.

Opposite page:

See you later, alligator!

44

Skilled Survivors

Alligators may look and sometimes act threatening, but people have little real reason to fear them. In fact, an alligator will go out of its way to avoid people and will not knowingly attack a human being unless it is provoked or cornered. And, as we have seen, the alligator's appearance and behavior are ideally suited to its way of life as a cold-blooded reptile, hunter and swimmer.

The alligator's skill as a hunter and the incredible story of its youthful struggle to survive should win our admiration, not our fear. Let us hope that as more is known about this remarkable animal, fantastic stories will be replaced by far more interesting facts.

Special Words

Cold-blooded   Term used for animals that have no automatic internal control of their body temperature.

Crocodilians   Family of reptiles that includes alligators and crocodiles.

Egg tooth   A hard point on the tip of a baby alligator's nose which it uses to break its way out of its shell.

Lagoon   Pond or small lake connected with a larger body of water.

Marsh   A flat area of land covered with shallow water.

Mate   To come together to produce young.

Naturalist   A person who studies nature.

Nostrils   The openings that allow air into the nose.

Predator   Animal that hunts other animals for food.

Prey   An animal hunted by another animal for food.

Reptile   Class of cold-blooded animals that includes snakes, alligators, turtles and lizards.

Scale   Thin, hard plates that form the outer layer of the alligator's skin.

INDEX

Cover Photo: Stephen J. Krasemann (Valan Photos)
Photo Credits: Stephen J. Krasemann (Valan Photos), pages 4, 15, 33; Bill Ivy,
page 7; Kennon Cooke (Valan Photos), pages 8, 12; J. D. Taylor (Miller
Services), page 16; Robert C. Simpson (Valan Photos), page 21; Barry Ranford,
page 22; John Fowler (Valan Photos), page 25; Norman Lightfoot (Eco-Art
Productions), pages 26, 37; J. D. Markou (Miller Services), page 29; C. P.
George (Miller Services), page 30; Harold Lambert (Miller Services), page 34;
J. A. Wilkinson (Valan Photos), page 38; Harold V. Green (Valan Photos),
pages 41, 45; Guy Lebel (Valan Photos), page 42.